Contents

Chapter 1: Achievement and Wealth Strategies 2
Chapter 2: Your vision of a millionaire 7
Chapter 3: Making your millionaire vision a reality! 13
Chapter 4: Your plan to become a millionaire 19
Chapter 6: Attaining your purpose 28
Chapter 7: Increase your influence 36
Chapter 8: Final Word 39

Chapter 1: Achievement and Wealth Strategies

The first step to getting to be rich is to figure out how to increase riches. The most progressive approach to assemble riches is to pick up abilities and utilize and charge individuals for administrations or from an item you have made. To increase riches, you should escape the corporate attitude of just continue working for another person. For those not keen on entrepreneurial desires, there are still choices to procure riches. A few people are not well off because they don't know how to end up rich and have the wrong view of how to procure more riches. **I will teach you ways on how to build and achieve wealth over the long-term:**

How to build Wealth from nothing:
1. Create a small reserve account ($1000-$2000)
2. Create a larger reserve account (at least half a year of expenses)
3. Pay off all or most debts, from the smallest to the largest
4. Invest in retirement accounts (10-15% of salary at minimum)
5. Begin a higher education fund for your children (if any) while investing commercial or personal property
6. Invest assets that generate cash –flow income to achieve financial freedom

Assuming if you live with a partner, have 2 incomes to live off one income and pay debt down with the other then begin investing

Fill up the timeline to keep track of your plan!

Timeline	Start Date	End Date
1. Create a small reserve account ($1000-$2000)		
2. Create a larger reserve account (at least half a year of expenses)		
3. Pay off all or most debts, from the smallest to the largest		
4. Invest in retirement accounts (10-15% of salary at minimum)		
5. Begin a higher education fund for your children (if any) while investing commercial or personal property		
6. Invest assets that generate cash-flow income to achieve financial freedom		

Wealth and Prosperity Habits:
1. Wake up early: Get more hours out of the day than the average person
2. Take calculated risks when investing or entrepreneurship
3. Work on other ventures while you are working
4. Read books every month about success, finance, and wealth building
5. Have the urgency to act on opportunities
6. Sacrifice your life, family, and friends to work towards your vision
7. Find a millionaire advisor to learn from
8. Join or start a group who is on its way to accomplish similar goals
9. Do not stop working on something when you are exhausted

10. Stay or become healthy by watching what you eat and exercising daily

Daily Routine of the wealthy:
1. Rise early in the morning, or two hours before regular wake up schedule to read the information in your field or about subjects related to where you are intending to go in
2. Make a list of everything you need to do that day
3. Prioritize the list in order of importance
4. Start on the most important thing in the list with concentration, focus, and discipline. Then go to the next one after completion
5. Listen to audio programs or books during travelling
6. After experiences reflect what did I do right? What would I differently next time? Then write down how to improve
7. Maximize your way to finding a solution to a problem. For instance, how do I double my income in less than 3 years? Write out 20 ways to accomplish this or solutions then act on them

Fill up your priority list and reflect on them!

Order of Importance	Activity	Start Time	End Time	Reflections

Ways to earn a second income! Act on your plans!

1. **Rental**: If you rent out a home, apartment, or commercial real estate, your clients will pay you to rent each month regardless of how you spend your time
2. **Software**: accumulate money with coding over the Internet. This could be anything from financial software to an iPhone/Alexa app
3. **Content**: Offering data could mean you run a daily paper or a magazine. It could likewise imply that you're a creator or a blogger. Compose and create data items, make physical items, counsel and charge expenses, blogging, internet business store, money related administrations, for example, impose arrangement, and land administration.
4. **Distribution**: Delivering products and services to large populations. Some people desire to create the product or information while others desire to get it out to the world such as food delivery
5. **Human resource**: Having employees to run the company for you.
6. **Financial Instruments:** Producing income-generating assets that are more than your expenses. These financial instruments produce

dividends for the investor. This meant financial freedom and/or retirement.

Changing your mindset!

Here, it is imperative that whatever activity you have should be a stepping stone to enable you to accomplish more. The goal is to set aside extra cash for future speculations, business possession, land or any such asset that produces salary. When you work in most corporate companies, you have an upper cap on your pay. The general population who end up extraordinary are not tied down by occupations but are engaged in different wage streams and ventures. Employment will never pay what one is worth, so it is imperative to go out and make your own particular benefits. Disappointment can't terrify you and assumes a part in your general achievement. You don't wind up awesome by simply working an 8 to 5 work at that point resigning and afterward biting the dust. Individuals who wind up an extraordinary pass on their insight and knowledge and leave monstrous measures of impact that empowers others. To achieve an accomplishment as far as riches, you should figure your life, and you do that by investing energy with one's self to reveal ways that produce cash.

Chapter 2: Your vision of a millionaire

My sole opinion is that people with a vision are successful, thought-provoking, and inspirational people. A vision demonstrates a purpose and gives a person a "why." The "why" is used often today in messages intending to uncover the reasons we do things and the motivation behind our actions. Here, I will focus on a person's vision and how to make it a reality.

1. **Write it out on paper:** This helps your brain remember.
2. **Hang up your vision**: Where it can be seen constantly, this puts positive pressure on you to carry out your vision.
3. **Make an outline with a timeline:** The outline consists of an approach to achieving your vision. A step by step guide that makes it simple and breaks down the actions that go toward the vision. In addition, the outline also has notes and things to remember and even who to contact. Along with who to contact other things include but are not limited to: where to go to get the information needed, how to acquire useful resources, what to do when there is an obstacle in the way. The timeline comes into play so there is a measure of

when things should be done, so you can hold yourself accountable for the steps getting done in a timely manner. Having a timeline is good but is also going to shape the way you handle or juggle objectives that need to become complete.
4. **Making it real!** After your vision is clear and the outline and timeline are completed then the transitional part begins and moves the vision into reality and is brought to life.

I challenge my readers to think bigger than what you are accustomed to, create and implement your own vision. What scares many people is the possibility of failure. No one wants to fail or be looked upon as a failure but what you do not often hear from the great successors is that they have failed miserably numerous times before their big break to success.

Quote of the Chapter: A dying person's biggest fear is that they will die knowing that they accomplished little to nothing or that they left with no vision or a purpose completed meaningfully.

Whether a person's idea is innovative or basic, it is stressful and hard if you do not focus on the vision. What happens is that if you have an idea to become a business owner and never make a business outline or any plan, then it brings up the question how serious and how hard did you really want to start a business. A serious person about business not only makes a business outline but are raising money for startup cost and trying to contact the right people to fulfill business goals.

You will find that simple, easy steps or tactics play a huge role in empowering or keeping you focused on the vision. If a person has a vision written down but without any time-specific accounts of when events take place, it is difficult moving forward.

The average person sees something so much, then it becomes a priority. You will begin to carry out the steps that will contribute to your vision. This is completely relevant to the drive to become a millionaire because millionaires have a vision then they execute it. The best things to do in approaching your vision is to become consistent and relentless until your vision is met.

The person who wins is the one who endures until the very end. When it comes to the topic of purposefulness or vison-making ideas, many commoners escape from it or do not put in maximum effort. This is because it is much easier living with no purpose because nothing is expected of you. It is much easier to wake up and do nothing and just live and breathe with no strong pursuit of a real desire. However, when you make a vision clear, whether to yourself or others, you now have expectations

I often hear people say, "allow yourself to converse and hang around successful people". It is hard because sometimes you do not know where these people are and may need to look them up. If not, please re-evaluate what needs work so that your vision is always at work and in progress. Visions grow and maybe even change but always remember to hard and remain strong through obstacles of hardship.

Holding yourself accountable and or having another person hold you to your vision may produce good results. This allows people or a person to continually check on you for updates to see what progress you have made. On the negative side, it can become embarrassing if no progress is made or if the person holding you accountable does not follow through with checkups. The choice is yours. For me, I prefer to hold myself accountable.

Many of my mind-blowing revealing ideas had occurred when I was alone. People are afraid to be alone that sometimes you cannot think clearly enough to pursue an idea until you have been alone. Visionaries often take on a lot of pressure if people know what they are trying to achieve and well many will not believe in you however they do not decide your fate. In the past, I doubted myself often and could never find confidence in performing a job. Doubt stems from many things, including the fear of failing. The bridge to a person's vision becoming a reality is not always at the very end of their success but is made real through the pain and obstacles they overcome to reach the highest point in your life.

We must get over this fear of failing and looking bad among others. You would not believe how many do not achieve greatness because they believe it is not possible or it is simply that they never act on it or even if acted upon after a few attempts if failed ones a person gives up.

We must become warriors and refuse to lose on this journey toward greatness. believe our human existence is much more than just being average but is something much more. We all are here to uplift, captivate, inspire, influence, and excel to such a level that it is not only remarkable but groundbreaking to even world-changing. Once the vision is clear and as you work to accomplish it to make it real you are becoming or rather in the process of being great. Moving forward another critical step taking it a step further the just the vision is the execution of the vision.

Chapter 3: Making your millionaire vision a reality!

It is common to not have a vision but also common to have a vision but no direction or guide to execute a plan that completes a vision. The execution should open the doors to lay a pathway to your desired vision. Execution is the physical action that takes place to land you where you want to go. These are your attempts and activities that you conduct that ultimately lead to your success in greatness.

The ultimate course of action to make your millionaire dream a reality:

1. **Know what is required to carry out your vision**

Do you need certain experience, certifications, or skill of any sort? Once this is understood then plan to develop are increase your skills or experience in that area. When acquiring the required tools, skills, or experience, it is important you do more than what is required.

The best decision you can make is when you invest in yourself. When you put time into yourself and pursues as hard as you can, you will become great. Your success is often determined by your preparation work. Ask yourself how many books or sources important to your vision's success have you read? Are you discussing these topics with experts? Are you acting on things that bring you closer to your vision?

If you find yourself stuck, you must find out a way to overcome this obstacle, so you do not remain in the same place. Overcome this! Since when is attaining greatness easy? If it is easy, then everyone will achieve it.

2. Position yourself to achieve those requirements

If you already have met the requirements, you will design a way to advance yourself in that expertise at such a level that your ability far exceeds the average person. To execute a plan for your vision after knowing what is required to obtain it now is to equip yourself. By equipping yourself, you allow yourself to meet the expectations or qualifications of your desired vision.

3. Put your expertise into practice

Put your expertise into practice and have a way to measure if your actions directly impacted your vision. By making yourself prepared for your vision, you are showing that you are serious. Many people will have a vision but never act on it. Therefore, the ones that distinguish themselves are the ones that plan and equip the knowledge and resources together to establish their foundation and roadmap to pursue the vision. When making sure you have the right knowledge or resources a good way to start is to learn the basics of what is needed from you. If certain skills or experience are required, make sure to master them and invest in yourself the most. When you invest in yourself that could mean anything but for now generally it means researching, planning, and acting on the plans you outlined all the way until your vision is complete.

4. **Learn from advisors and experts in your field of interest**

As you execute your vision by allowing yourself to be equipped, it is important to find advisors or experts in that field. These people may be hard to contact but with reasonable consistent attempts, you may get a chance to ask questions about your game plan. This will expose you to more information and possible resources that could play a role in your success.

If people are not responding after you reach out, try others. There are good sources online, so you should consider writing an email or calling their offices. If you are new in a subject that you are trying to learn, you should know the bare minimum about your subject of interest before you talk to them.

5. Be Professionally presentable

After you make the connections, you need to market themselves well enough to be professionally presentable. This allows others to view you in a positive yet unique way. Make them remember your niche and your vision.

• **Dress the part**: have the proper attire for the right occasion or opportunity. Although people tend to associate that with business attire, dressing the part is actually dependent on the environment a person is entering into.

• **Be consistent in your marketing approach**: Market **your personal brand** will allow people to see you in what you want over time. If you love to wear nice and stylish clothes, then people will know that you have good quality in clothes selection. You can then offer help to others by choosing a style of clothing wear that fits them.
You may be surprised by how well a person carries themselves how far they make it in life in simple but effective ways. If your pursuit is relentless enough in advancing your personal brand in a healthy way, then

patience is the key. Patience is necessary all while you reach a point where you are trusted and revered as a person who is of good character.

6. Always be prepared for any and every moment

Now it is time to perform. You should successfully act on a task and get it well done. Therefore, you must prepare in advance for your big break or opportunity. Preparation for success and for your vision is a part of the equation now you must perform well once your chance comes up.

7. Stay positive even when you have made mistakes that hurt your personal brand.

It can become difficult to perform in some cases because of hostile or negative environments. This, however, should not discourage you from advancing. You must believe in preparing as hard as you can by practicing.

8. Recover quickly and wisely from missed opportunities.

When you start a business and if it fails, you must still believe that you are a successful business person. Even if everyone gives up on you, you must believe that you can make your vision a reality. It is a hard truth but sometimes pain from failure helps a person to succeed. It is important that once the vision is created, you pursue it relentlessly and do not stop until it happens. The execution of your vision is critical because this is the bridge that one crosses that brings your vision to reality.

When your moment comes, what will you do? Will you seize the moment and get out of everything you want, or will you let it fade away into the darkness? Your vision can act as a powerful tool for yourself to reach greater heights and travel to places you never knew existed. Your final piece in executing your vision is performance.

9. **Create and maintain professional relationships** with recruiters, hiring committees, and people who are deciding your job, school, or any group.

Quote of the chapter: be patient and let things come into place or position smoothly not roughly or forced.

Chapter 4: Your plan to become a millionaire

I will describe a basic approach to building a business plan for potential startups, new businesses, and existing ones which are looking forward to improving their business. This is related to greatness as you start a way to help build your own financial independence in the future. This business plan is subject to possible failure but if a failure occurs, adjustments should become made. Your relentless pursuit should remain in striving to build a successful business.

When you write your business plan, you do not need to stick to the exact business plan outline. Instead, use the sections that make the most sense for your business and your needs.

The 9 common sections are:

1. **Executive Writeup**

Tell your reader briefly what your company is and why it will be successful. Write your mission statement, your product or service, and basic information about your company's leadership team, employees, and location. If you plan to ask for financing or angel investment, you should also include financial information and high-level growth plans.

2. Company Description

Go into detail about the problems your business solves or the niche your business fills. Be specific by listing the target consumers, organizations your company plans to serve. Explain the competitive advantages of your business over others. Are there experts on your team? Have you found the perfect location for your store? Your company description is the place to boast about your strengths.

3. Market Analysis

You will need a good understanding of your industry outlook and target market. Competitive research will show you what your competitors are doing and what their strengths are. What are the trends and themes? What do successful competitors do? Why does it work? Can you do it better?

4. Organization and Management

Describe how your company will be structured and who will run it. Are you a general or limited partnership, or if you are a sole proprietor or LLC? Use an organizational chart to show who oversees what in your company. Show how each person's unique experience will contribute to the success of your venture, by including CVs of key members of your team.

5. Service or product line

Describe what you sell or what service you offer. Explain how it benefits your customers and what the product lifecycle looks like. Also share your plans for the intellectual property, such as copyright or patent filings. If you are doing research and development for your service or product, explain it in detail.

6. Marketing and Sales

You need to describe how you will attract and retain customers, down to the point of how a sale will actually happen. There is no single way to approach a marketing strategy. Your strategy should evolve and change to fit your unique needs. Make sure that you describe your complete marketing and sales strategies thoroughly, especially when you make financial projections.

One tactic is to use a social media platform such as Facebook or Google ads to specifically target potential customers. Another tactic is to formulate a sales team to find new businesses and retain current customers. You can also employ affiliate marketing to enable other businesses and brands to sell your products while they collect commissions.

7. Request for Funding

If you are asking for funding, you must outline your funding requirements. Your goal is to clearly explain how much funding you will need over the next five years and what it is to be used for. Give a detailed description of how you intend to use the funds. Specify if you need funds to buy equipment or materials, pay salaries, or cover specific bills until revenue increases. Always include a description of your future strategic financial plans, such as paying off debt or selling your business.

8. Financial projections

Supplement your funding request with financial projections. You must convince the investor that your business is stable and will be a financial success. If your business is already established, including income statements, balance sheets, and cash flow statements for the last three to five years. If you have other collaterals you could put against a loan, list it now.

Provide a prospective financial outlook for the next five years by adding forecasted income statements, balance sheets, cash flow statements, and capital expenditure budgets. For the first year, be even more specific and use quarterly or even monthly projections. Clearly explain your projections. The top tip is to use graphs and charts to tell the financial story of your business.

9. Appendix

Use your appendix to provide supporting documents or other materials that were specially mentioned, such as credit histories, resumes, product pictures, letters of reference, licenses, permits, or patents, legal documents, permits, and other contracts.

Chapter 5: Study! Study! Study!

Education is the backbone of a person's success and is the driving force propelling a person's vision. You can become knowledgeable in more than one area of study. You do not need to be limited to the traditional way of higher education or anything beyond a high school diploma. Any form of learning that is effective can increase your knowledge.

An obvious way of attaining an education is what many do, which is to go to school like a college, university or any such educational facility. These facilities usually offer degree programs and others certain certifications in a specific field. Regardless of what education endeavors you choose it is critical because the knowledge you acquire is what allows you to implement your ideas to practical actions in the real world. Also, education is not only traditional institutes but could refer to gaining or enhancing trade skills or anything that is used as an asset to generate wealth. Some would say that education is the trigger that ignites a movement that explores limitless theories and testes numerous ideas to uncover and find the truth and improve our livelihoods.

Access to education has been made more available, and opportunities for professional growth are at our fingertips. The question is to figure out what educational pathway is right for ourselves. Furthermore, we should find out what educational pathway is appropriate for our vision's success. There are many roads to a solid education. Choosing can prove difficult. It is worthwhile to find the education that is most closely related to your vision and often time your vision is sometimes also your passion.

Reasons why Education for you is important:

1. **Money**

An educated person has more chances of landing up a good high paying job. Money is important for survival in today's world. The more educated you are, the better career prospects you have!

2. **For a stable life with financial freedom**

If you want to lead a happy life and enjoy the good things the world has to offer, you certainly need to get educated and achieve financial freedom.

3. **Turns your dreams into reality**

What is your dream, your aim in life? Do you want to become rich? Do you want to be popular? Do you want to be an extremely successful person who is respected by people? Well, the key to all this is education.

4. Offers you self-dependence

Education is very important if you want to be an independent person. Education also makes you wiser so that you can make your own decisions.

5. Gives you confidence

Your educational degree is proof of your knowledge by society. If you are educated, you have more chances of being heard and taken seriously. Generally, an uneducated man will find it harder to express his views and opinions owning to lack of confidence. Even if he does so, people may not take him seriously. Hence, education gives you the confidence to express your views and opinions.

6. Gives you an equal footing

Education is a must if you wish to eliminate the existing differences between different social classes and genders. It opens a whole world of opportunities for the poor or women so that they are empowered to have an equal shot at well-paying jobs.

7. Saves you from being cheated

Education saves you from being exploited and fooled, such as signing false documents.

Chapter 6: Attaining your purpose

Self-purpose allows you to live in such a way it allows you to feel fulfilled in life. You should maximize your purpose in life. As crazy as this may sound because someone is making lots of money, it does not necessarily mean they are living in their purpose. Let us not use wealth as an indicator of a person living in their purpose.

Self-purpose comes from within. Only you can feel the feeling of fulfillment that others cannot feel for you. Some may claim they can sense or tell but that is through their own judgment. The ultimate judge is yourself and the feelings you have. If you are unsure, list ways to approach finding your self-purpose. Additionally, often when living in your purpose, whether you achieve your vision or not, you must develop your legacy. Legacy and self-purpose are closely related, even in wealth.

How to find your self-purpose?

Meditation allows you to unlock and uncover more about yourself and the direction you are headed in. It empowers strong conscious self-thoughts and a way to see more of your inner self. If you have no knowledge of what or how to meditate it is a good idea to research about meditation and find what methods would increase your ability to get the most out of it. What I did was create a purpose or a goal before each time I meditated so that way once I finished I had good outcomes or good insights into how I would shape my own future to live in my purpose. Meditation helped me clear my thoughts and concentrate on a bigger picture of life. Meditating is necessary if you want to speed up results and uncover or expand your purpose.

You need to search for ideas or opportunities until you uncover what fulfills and gives you a self-purposeful feeling. Take a person who has a special need relative and struggles to take care of relative but has a burning interest in helping and developing ways to give the best care to special needs people. This person begins ethically, responsibly, and legally creating or modifying theories, systems, or practices to aid special needs people in their day to day lives. Once successful and if ideas produce results this person's work reaches greater audiences or people who also would like to know how to best help special needs people. How great would this special need innovator feel after others see that his methods are effective and lasting? This gives the person a great sense of self-purpose and feels that their work is meaningful and purposeful. Also, when searching out ideas or opportunities to find your purpose it may or may not be in the field you are in which is the point of searching through ideas and finding the right opportunity that leads to your purpose. This example acts as a guide to help you see how people uncover their purpose or live in ways that are fulfilling. It is my hope that you will find ways to uncover your own purpose or expand your purpose if you have already found it. Expanding your purpose is critical as it increases its reach in your life you previously thought to be limited. By scaling your purpose, you increase your exposure and work with more people.

How does self-purpose relate to wealth?

You should by now feel a burning and undying energy that catapults you to break the financial boundaries in life that have once held you back. When self-purpose is used to accumulate wealth, it can become an unstoppable force.

Having a business is my greatest recommendation for building wealth. It is nice if a person can sell their way to a million with their business and live their purpose. Even if your purpose is not to create wealth, you should pursue it anyway because if you are able to make lots of money, you can use the money you earn to shape your future and explore finding your purpose with everything else taken care financially. It was self-purpose seeking that led many millionaires to their fortune.

Refuse to be average

If you are in a position where you do not have much money, you must believe that you can find a way out and let your self-purpose seeking lead you into a direction of discovering your purpose. This is not something that can be taught. How can one expect to be great if they do average things that make you an average person? Refuse to be average and refuse to let your circumstances prevent you from rising to greatness. The millionaire mindset is about turning your life purpose into reality yet take failures and setbacks as stepping stones to reach new heights. The millionaire mindset will unlock your untapped potential or grow your eagerness to chase your dreams.

What are you waiting for?
You do not become great by waiting. It is by action. What are you afraid of? Just go out and do it. Expect to fail (because you will!) but note that with each failure brings you closer to success. The millionaire mindset is embedded with tears of struggle, pain from major loses and heartache from disappointments. However, it is filled with an aspiring light and a direction that transforms you

into self-purposeful living. More than often, you need to motivate yourself because others may not.

In summary, you must:

- Aggressively read about finance, entrepreneurship, investing, and money management
- Set realistic goals, write them down with deadlines and deliverables
- Live, eat, sleep and shit business and wealth
- Become experts in marketing and sales
- Stay motivated and positive after countless rejections and failures
- Produce solutions and sell them

I must emphasize that there is no single way to financial independence but here you will see a series of ways from different lifestyles to gain financial freedom.

1. Start small

Read books on entrepreneurship and you will find ways to start a small business which does not even require upfront costs. Examples are like becoming an author and creating informational products that solve problems. I learned in marketing modules that many people buy those products as they relieve their problems and pain. You do not have to be an expert - you can simply compile research information then interpret it, find trends, simplify it, then sell it on digital platforms. The concept here is to find something, or if you already know your skill, profit from it.

Hence, you should take a calculated risk so that it will not hurt you in a way that would make you homeless or of anything detrimental. For low-income people, it is wise to have or start a business with low or no startup cost. It may be one of the most challenging things you have done or ever will do in life. If your funds are limited, try businesses that allow you to provide a solution or service, so you can make money without losing money. Well, you just only give up time.

If you need help, ask. Businesses like Indeed and Monster, are all businesses that connect job seekers with businesses and business pay them to find talent. Or other businesses such as eBay or Amazon that connects people wanting to sell their items to consumers. The point is to produce a marketplace that is efficient and effective in helping others connect for whatever purpose it may be.

2. **Real Estate**

Real estate and owning property is necessary, as they produce income continuously. Save money (15% to 20%) to make a purchase. Rent it out in a way that the total rent charged is greater than the total expenses such as maintenance and insurance. This is, in fact, the most important and easiest step to bring you closer toward building wealth.

3. Investment Products

Investment vehicles, such as stocks, bonds, mutual funds, can produce more money but always comes with risk. This form of wealth-building is often liquid which means you put your money in but you can also withdraw it quickly. You need to be careful because of the risk that you may lose more than you invest. You do not just pick randomly there is a tactic for these types of investing. The simplest thing to do is read and select investments that suit you the best. There are numerous ways people have benefited from these investments. Hopefully, more people are motivated to pursue it now. It is sad and depressing when people work a lifetime and have nothing to show.

4. Commodities

A commodity is a simple good used in a market, such as Metals (gold, silver, platinum), Energy (crude oil, heating oil, natural gas, gasoline), Livestock and Meat (live cattle, feeder cattle) and Agricultural (corn, soybeans, wheat, rice, cocoa, coffee, cotton, sugar,) Note that there are also risks to. Hence, wealth is not accumulated randomly, but only through careful choice of investments. Do not expect to put money into a random commodity thinking you will be rich. You can either buy physical amounts of raw commodities, future contracts or exchange-traded index products. More information about creating and developing ways to invest come from research and experience along with consulting with investing professionals.

Chapter 7: Increase your influence

Influence is what we can do to others in a positive way. When you influence someone, they can choose to make better decisions about their life. It should be something you should work for not only to reach success but to embark on a journey to establish ourselves as an influential character. Anyone can influence others. A person's influence on another can break boundaries such as doubt of success. It is something inspirational when a person is positively influenced by you. That person gains confidence and starts to make changes in their lifestyle which brings them closer to greatness.

The connection between Influence and Wealth

People who become wealthy always empowers and give a greater impact on their followers. More often than not, even if he/she is not wealthy yet, a person with good or rising influence will be likely to become wealthy. If you have 100,000 followers, because of something unique like you, sing well or any skill, on YouTube, social media, or any medium that allows people to follow you, that presents an opportunity to retain and expand your influence.

How to gain influence

Start simple by using your talent to reach others. Find areas where you can place your talent in front of others. If you are an author, write books in any literary form, then have book events. If you are unknown, promote yourself by giving free books away to set up the audience and potential buyers of your next book. If you are a good presenter give free speeches about any subject of interest to any community. Regardless of what talent or gist you have, you must influence and use selling techniques to build wealth. As you move up to the national and international realms of influence, the number of people you influence increase dramatically. It is likely to produce more revenue and profits. Once you have the influence, it can become easier to sell to those who have been influenced or develop solutions that they are willing to pay for. Marketing whether business or in a way to promote yourself in non-business ways what is a way to go about it and succeed in attaining a high level of influence.

You can gain influence by:

1. **Creation**

One must develop or alter something legally that currently exists to make it your own. Let people know the product or service is in the motion of being created, so as to create the hype leading up to its official date of release or servicing.

Assuming if you have little to no budget, it is best to use word of mouth techniques like tell others and offer free items that cost no money or little to get people attention. Most people will accept free items even if they do not utilize them. You can also volunteer to present yourself to others or spread the word to gain influence.

2. Present

You need to take your creation and get it in front of people. Unless you have the budget to pay, social media and email outreach are necessary. Everyone you come in contact with must know of your created product or service. This will maximize your appearance. Do not rest until every ounce of your time is focused on getting in front of others whether is it locally or internationally. Those who succeed try and fail then adopt and become creative until a trend leads to more success.

3. Follow-up

You need to follow up with people who have bought from you to see what their feedback is. If there is a reward, all the better, as it sets up a chance to potentially sell again. You should not fear negative feedback as it provides you avenues on how to improve and sell better.

4. Growth

This is similar to point two in presenting yourself, but here numbers will be the primary goal. Increase your traffic by seeking out every avenue that is free, until they are exhausted. Afterward, set a course to become internationally renowned. Increase your visibility by creating partnerships with other companies via promotions, volunteering, and networking.

Chapter 8: Final Word

I know that you typically do not read this section, so I will present it in point form for easier digesting:

1. Define what success means to you and the type of successful life you desire to live. Make it plain and write it down and the steps broken up leading to that lifestyle.

2. Approach greatness by preparation and dedication to learning and improving every day through practical measures like reading.

3. Minimizes distractions, endures hardships and produces results under pressure.

4. Understand greatness is within your grasp but you must seek it out as if your life depended on it.

5. Make your vision reality by taking practical steps and not resting into it comes to fruition. Ideas and vision stay that way until actions are taken to fulfill them.

6. Get the Education necessary to excel and overcome any obstacle.

7. Have a clear purpose in why you are pursuing wealth, so as to keep motivated and driven to complete your purpose.

8. Build or create your sphere of influence, so that others continue your work through your legacy even after death.

Be a Master of your Fate!

www.ingramcontent.com/pod-product-compliance
Lightning Source LLC
Chambersburg PA
CBHW031556210526
45464CB00003B/1313